A MILLION DOTS

Andrew Clements
illustrated by Mike Reed

Simon & Schuster Books for Young Readers
New York   London   Toronto   Sydney

For Karen Bloom,
a friend and fellow teacher
—A. C.

To Jane, Alex, and Joe
—M. R.

SIMON & SCHUSTER BOOKS FOR YOUNG READERS
An imprint of Simon & Schuster Children's Publishing Division
1230 Avenue of the Americas, New York, New York 10020
Text copyright © 2006 by Andrew Clements
Illustrations copyright © 2006 by Mike Reed

SIMON & SCHUSTER BOOKS FOR YOUNG READERS is a trademark of Simon & Schuster, Inc.
Book design by Lucy Ruth Cummins
The text for this book is set in Chowderhead.
The illustrations for this book are rendered digitally.
Manufactured in China
2 4 6 8 10 9 7 5 3 1
Library of Congress Cataloging-in-Publication Data
Clements, Andrew, 1949-
A million dots / Andrew Clements ; illustrated by Mike Reed.
p. cm.
ISBN-13: 978-0-689-85824-6
ISBN-10: 0-689-85824-8
1. Million (The number)—Juvenile literature. I. Reed, Mike, 1951- ill. II. Title.
QA141.3.C54 2005
513.2'11—dc22
2004005349

first
edition

.

Look at the center of this page.
Right at the very center.
Look carefully.
That's one dot.
One dot is not very many.
It's only one, and that's just one more than none.

But look on this page.
This is ten dots.
. . . .

That's more than one, but it's still not so many.

And here is one hundred dots.

And here is five hundred dots.

And here is a thousand dots.

You probably think that a thousand dots starts to look like a lot of dots.
That's what I used to think too.
Then I saw a *million* dots.
And that's what you are going to do too. Right now.
Ready? Then jump to the bottom of this page and get going.
And don't forget to look at every single dot.
Just kidding about that.
Because if you took only *one second* to look at each dot, and you really did
look at all one million of them, how long would it take you to finish reading this book?
Eleven and a half days! Because a million is a *lot* of dots.
So don't stare at every single dot—unless you really want to.
But remember, you are actually going to *see* **ONE MILLION DOTS**.
And to get in the spirit, you can start counting all one million of them from
left to right and from top to bottom, beginning right here with
dot number **ONE**.

· ·

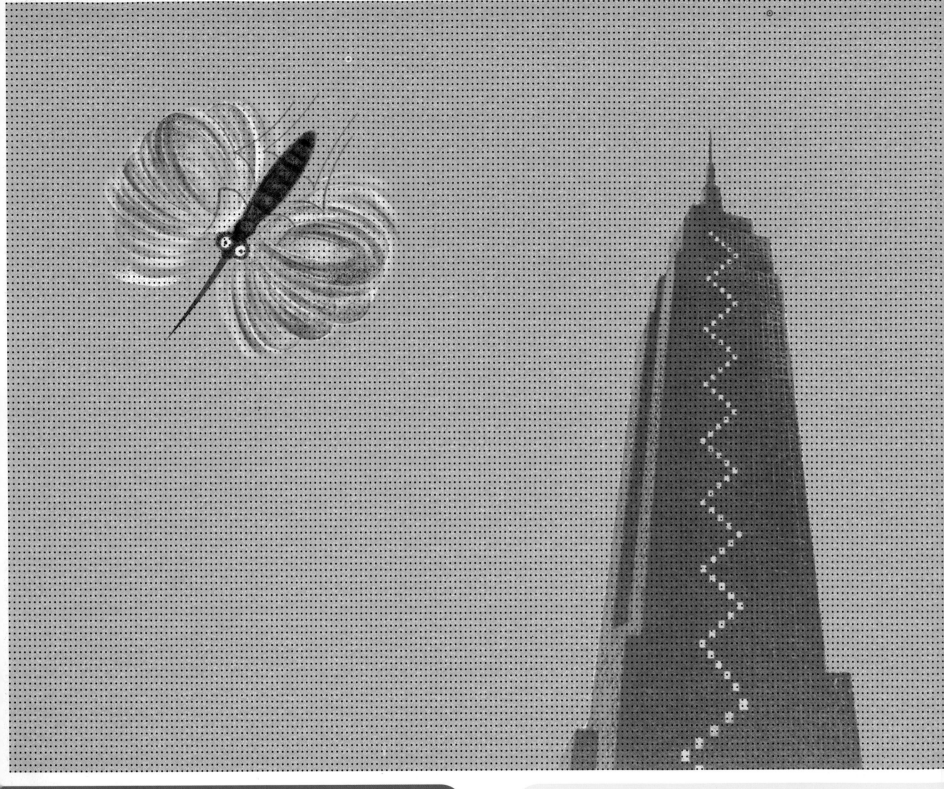

The wings of a mosquito beat 600 times each second.

A person must climb 1,860 steps to walk to the top of the Empire State Building.

It is 24,901 miles around the Earth at the equator.

47,679 dots so far

DOT NUMBER
66,660

Earth has traveled 66,660 miles in its orbit around the sun during the last hour.

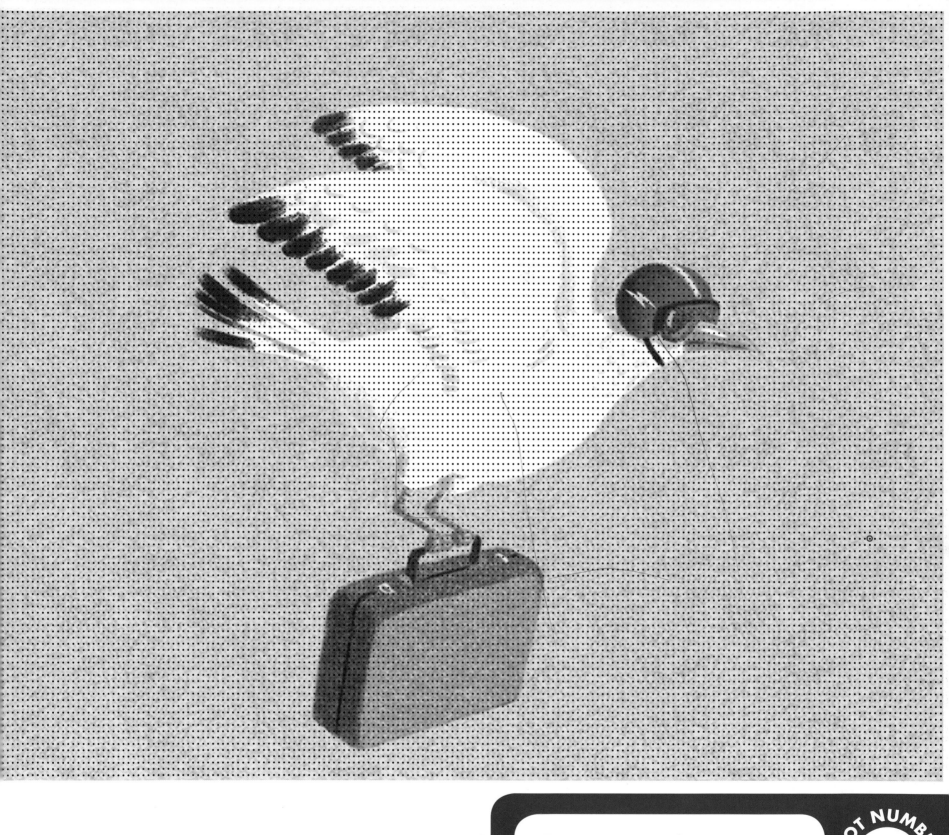

The sooty tern can fly nonstop for 87,600 hours after it leaves the nest—that's ten years on the wing!

DOT NUMBER
87,600

95,295 dots so far

DOT NUMBER
100,000

An adult sperm whale weighs as much as 100,000 pounds.

DOT NUMBER 133,381

The combined heights of the tallest mountains on each of the Earth's seven continents is 133,381 feet.

Mount Kosciusko, Australia, 7,310 feet
Mount Elbrus, Europe, 18,481 feet
Vinson Massif, Antarctica, 16,067 feet
Mount Kilimanjaro, Africa, 19,340 feet
Mount McKinley, North America, 20,320 feet
Mount Aconcagua, South America, 22,835 feet
Mount Everest, Asia, 29,028 feet

A person blinks about 134,000 times each week.

DOT NUMBER 134,000

142,911 dots so far

A queen-size bedsheet is woven from more than 153,000 feet of cotton thread.

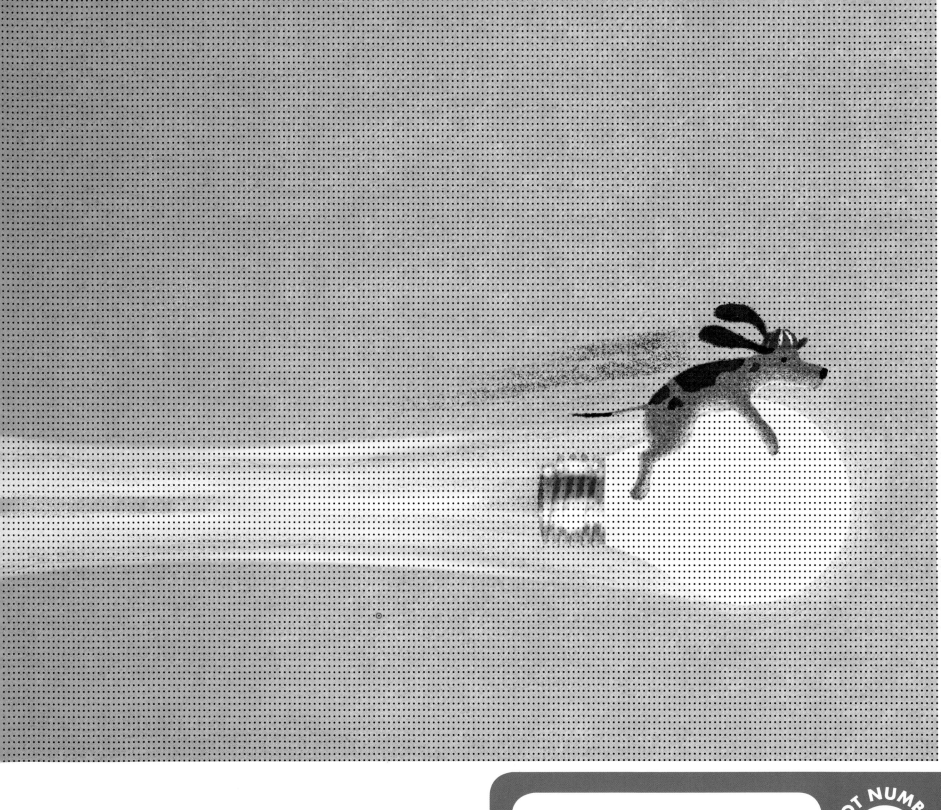

Light travels through space at about 186,000 miles per second.

DOT NUMBER
186,000

190,527 dots so far

200,000 pennies would fill twenty-two one-gallon milk jugs.

A stack of 232,224 shoe boxes would be three times taller than Mount Everest, the tallest mountain on Earth.

DOT NUMBER
232,224

238,143 dots so far

238,857

It's 238,857 miles from the Earth to the moon.

More than 265,000 different kinds of moths and butterflies live on Earth.

DOT NUMBER
265,000

285,759 dots so far

More than 300,000 different kinds of beetles live on Earth.

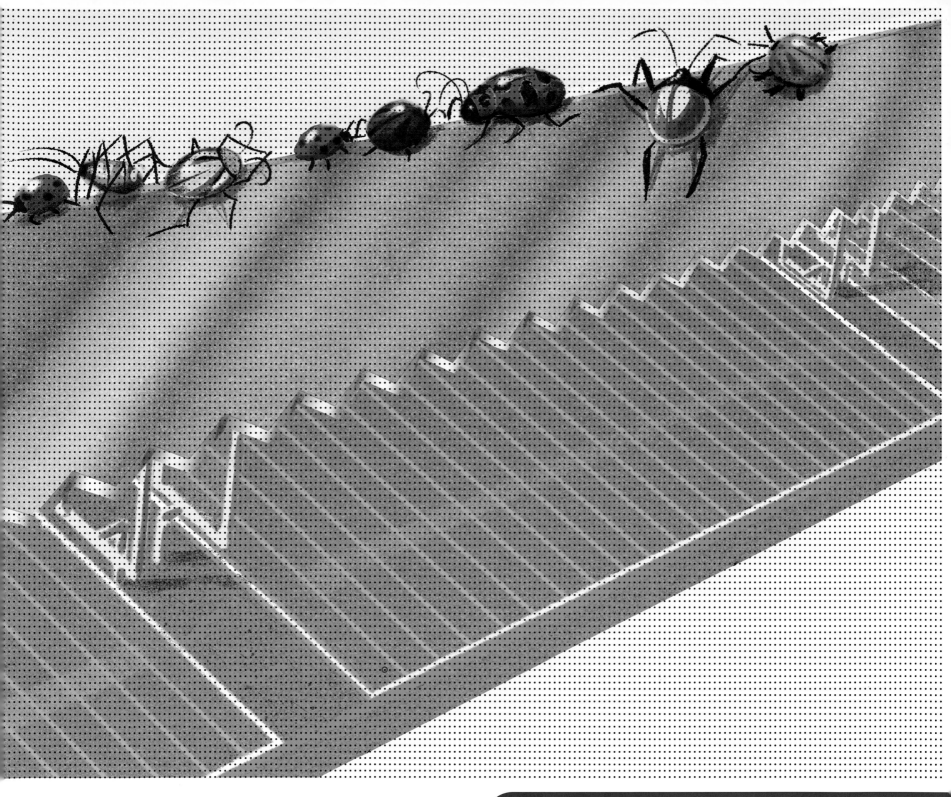

A carpenter's saw with 330,000 saw teeth would be longer than ten football fields.

DOT NUMBER
330,000

333,375 dots so far

DOT NUMBER 350,000

By the time a gray whale is twenty-nine years old—about half its life—it has already traveled more than 350,000 miles on its yearly migrations.

364,800 cans of soup would fill more than 950 grocery carts.

380,991 dots so far

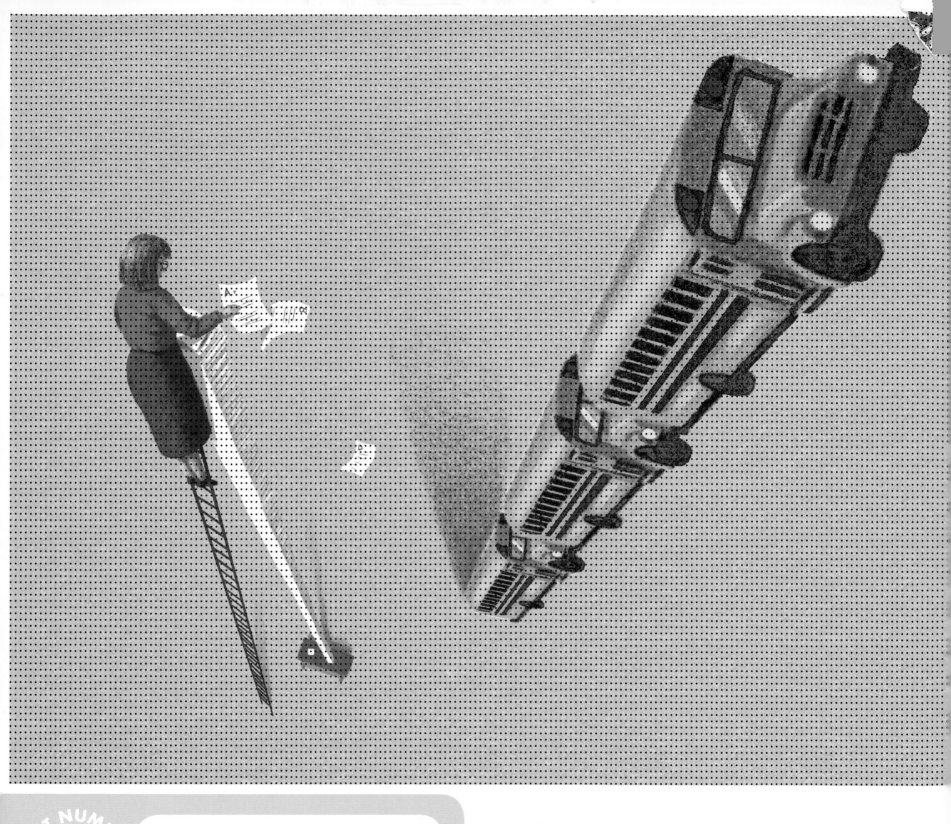

DOT NUMBER

385,500

If each of the 385,500 dots so far were one sheet of paper, all of them would make a stack 124 feet tall, almost as tall as three school buses balanced end-to-end.

Sir Arthur Conan Doyle used more than 416,000 words to tell forty-six of the best adventures of Sherlock Holmes. Read all forty-six, and you'll still have plenty of mystery left—more than 149,000 other words.

DOT NUMBER
416,000

428,607 dots so far

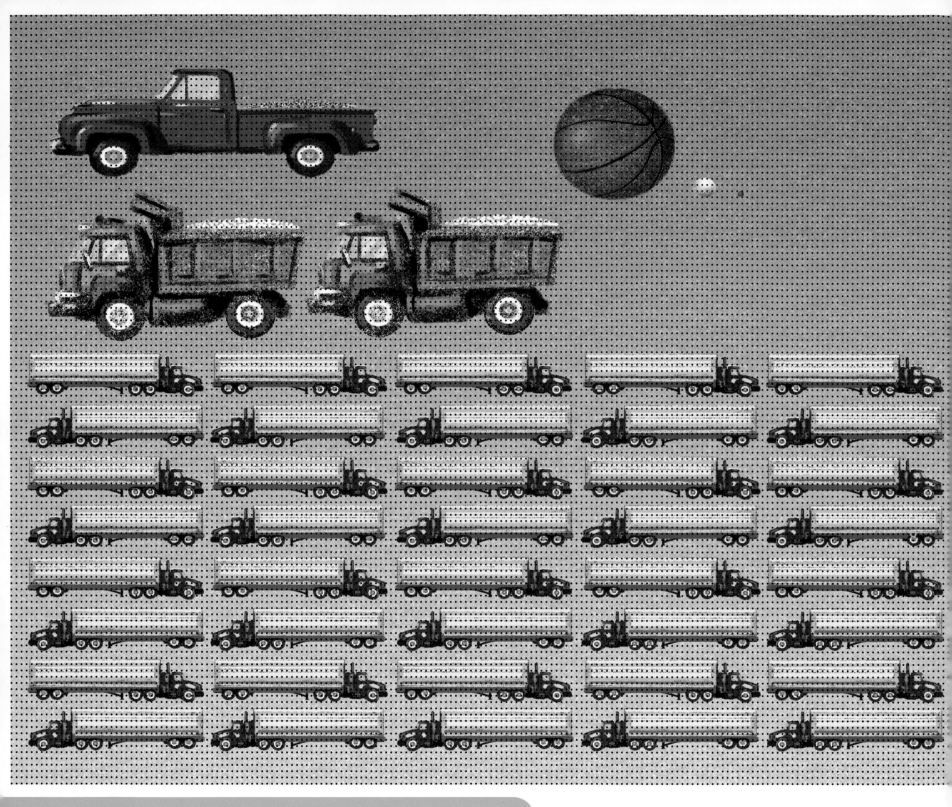

If each of the 444,768 dots so far was a gumball, you could put them into the back of a big pickup truck and give one to every man, woman, and child in Kansas City, Missouri (2003 figures). If you were giving out golf balls, you'd need two dump trucks. If you were handing out baseballs, you'd need two forty-foot semitrailers. And if you were passing out 444,768 basketballs, you'd need sixty-eight semitrailers to carry them all.

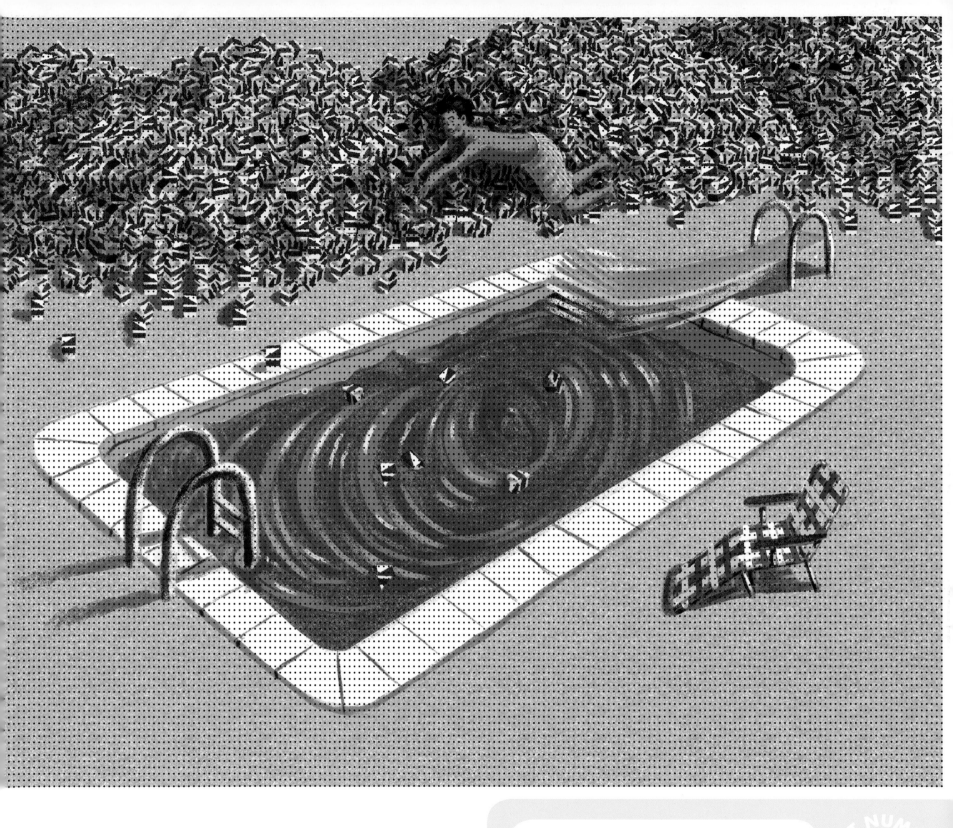

It would take 464,000 school-lunch cartons of chocolate milk to fill a 20-by-40-foot swimming pool. (Please pass the straws.)

DOT NUMBER
464,000

476,223 dots so far

More than 500,000 cars have been taken to junkyards in the United States during the past sixteen days.

The drum of a clothes dryer that dries only one load of laundry every day for one year will spin around more than 513,920 times.

DOT NUMBER
513,920

523,839 dots so far

DOT NUMBER
525,600

There are 525,600 minutes from one birthday to the next one.

There were 529,245 children born in California in the year 2002.

DOT NUMBER
529,245

Three ordinary wooden pencils can draw a line 554,000 feet—more than 100 miles!—long.

Tie 578,504 shoelaces together, and they would reach from New York to Boston.

More than 615,100 different words
are explained in the *Oxford English
Dictionary.*

615,100

619,071 dots so far

The *Knock Nevis*—the largest ship in the world—weighs 622,538 tons. The red mark shows how large a car would look on the ship's deck.

An arctic tern will fly more than 650,000 miles during its lifetime.

DOT NUMBER
650,000

666,687 dots so far

DOT NUMBER
675,000

Like chocolate? To eat 675,000 Hershey's bars, you would have to eat one bar every two minutes, nonstop, for more than 234 days!

An average person's heart beats about 700,000 times a week.

714,303 dots so far

Forty-five *Tyrannosaurus rex* dinosaurs would weigh about 720,000 pounds.

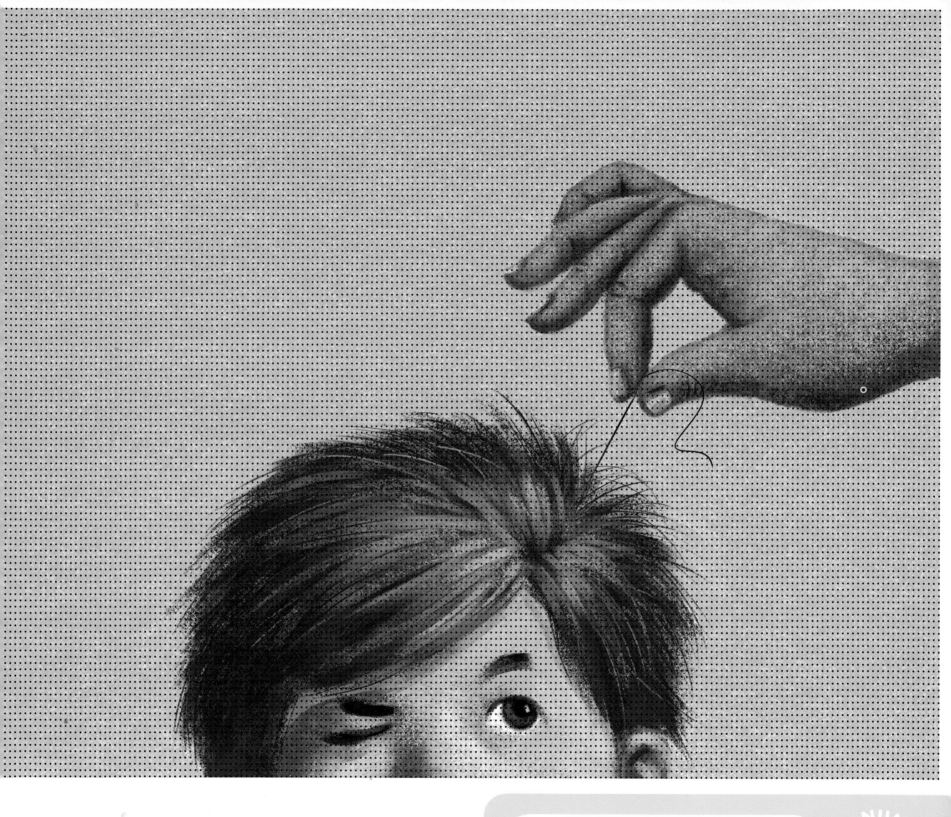

If you count every hair on the heads of five people, you'll find about 750,000 hairs.

More than 765,174 men and women work for the U.S. Postal Service, and on average they deliver more than 630 million cards, letters, magazines, catalogs, and parcels each day.

All the Silly Putty from 800,000 little red plastic eggs would make a coral-colored cube 7 feet 4 inches square, which would weigh 23,408 pounds—about as much as two large African elephants.

DOT NUMBER
800,000

809,535 dots so far

823,680 pieces of uncooked spaghetti laid on the ground side-by-side would make a brittle pasta path one mile long. Laid end-to-end, the same 823,680 pieces of spaghetti would stretch more than 129 miles!

If you brush your teeth about two minutes a day, during the past five years you've moved your toothbrush up and down and back and forth about 839,500 times.

DOT NUMBER
839,500

857,151 dots so far

The sun has a diameter of 864,948 miles—wide enough to fit 109 Earths.

902,400 apples would completely cover a basketball court three feet deep—and if the old saying is true, that many apples would keep the doctor away for more than 2,470 years!

DOT NUMBER
902,400

904,767 dots so far

DOT NUMBER
924,000

924,000 pencils stacked this way would make a tower of pencils more than two miles high.

942,500 playing cards spread out edge-to-edge would cover an entire football field, plus parts of each end zone. You would need 18,125 decks of cards.

DOT NUMBER
942,500

952,383 dots so far

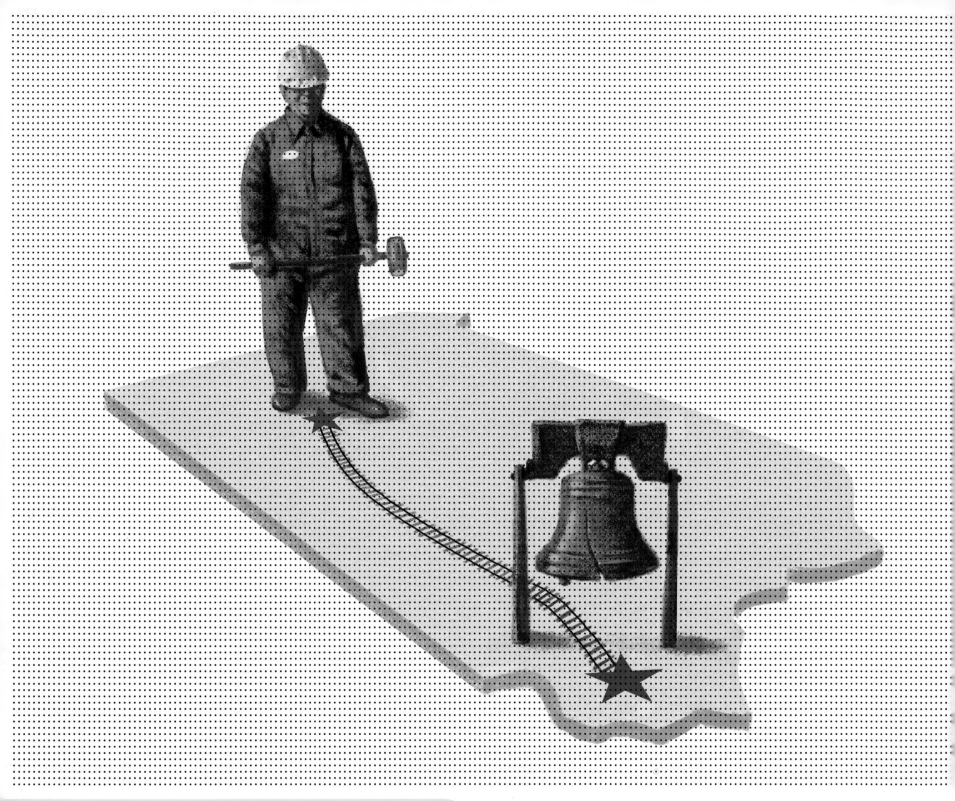

On just one set of railroad tracks between Philadelphia and Pittsburgh, Pennsylvania, more than 975,744 railroad ties are needed to hold the rails in place.

Because each second of a movie is made up of 24 separate pictures, there are a total of 996,480 still pictures in six of the most popular American movies ever made: *E.T. the Extra-Terrestrial, Jurassic Park, Star Wars, The Lion King, Forrest Gump,* and *Home Alone.*

DOT NUMBER
996,480

999,999 dots so far

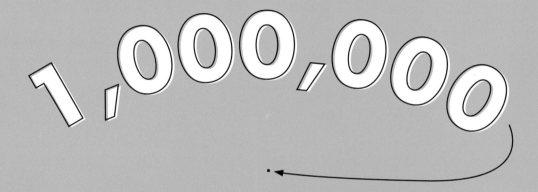

1,000,000

Like I said so many dots ago, a

MILLION

is a *lot* of dots!